Original title:
Warm Lights in Winter's Chill

Copyright © 2024 Creative Arts Management OÜ
All rights reserved.

Author: Alexander Thornton
ISBN HARDBACK: 978-9916-94-426-4
ISBN PAPERBACK: 978-9916-94-427-1

Light as a Beacon in the Abyss of Cold

In shadows deep where silence reigns,
A flicker bright breaks through the chains.
It dances soft on night's dark waves,
A guide for souls, the lost, the brave.

With gentle glow, it warms the air,
A whispered hope, a heartfelt prayer.
Through icy winds, its brilliance flows,
A compass true where courage grows.

Each flicker tells of battles won,
Of weary hearts, and dreams begun.
In darkest times, it lights the way,
A promise sung at break of day.

So hold it close in frigid night,
Let every spark ignite the fight.
For in the cold, we'll find our way,
With light as guide, we're here to stay.

Stars Behind Frosted Windows

Whispers of light through chilly panes,
Frosted patterns like delicate chains.
Twinkling dreams in the velvet night,
Stars behind windows, a comforting sight.

Silent tales in the icy glare,
Stories wrapped in the winter air.
Each shimmering orb a wish we share,
Brightened shadows, we stop and stare.

Luminous Nights of Solace

In the stillness, the stars ignite,
Guiding hearts through the endless night.
Soft glows breathe life into the dark,
Luminous nights, where hopes can spark.

Whispers of peace in the cool embrace,
Night wraps us in its gentle grace.
Each moment feels like a sacred dance,
In luminous nights, we find romance.

Radiance Amidst the Snow

Softly falling, the snowflakes gleam,
Blanketing earth, a winter dream.
Radiance brightens the frosty ground,
Nature's magic all around found.

Underneath the moon's watchful eye,
Sparkling crystals under the sky.
Whispers of warmth in chill's embrace,
In the snow's radiance, we find our place.

Candle Glow in Frozen Air

Candle flames flicker, a warm retreat,
Casting shadows, soft and sweet.
Flickering light in the frozen air,
A beacon of hope, a love we share.

In the solitude of winter's chill,
Heartfelt warmth, a comforting thrill.
Candle glow dances, bringing cheer,
In frozen moments, we hold dear.

Nestled Among the Chilled

Beneath the branches, shadows play,
The whispering winds, a soft ballet.
Frosty breaths in morning's glow,
Find the warmth in the cold below.

Nature's quilt, a blanket drawn,
Silvery threads, the waking dawn.
Stillness wraps the world so tight,
Nestled here till fades the night.

Glimmering Hopes Through Gloom

Amidst the shadows, stars ignite,
Flickering dreams take their flight.
Each tiny spark, a whispered cheer,
Glimmers of hope radiate near.

In the depths where darkness dwells,
A guiding light, the heart compels.
Embers of faith, brightening skies,
Through the gloom, the spirit flies.

Lanterns Amidst the White

Snowflakes dance in soft embrace,
Lanterns glow, a warming grace.
Guiding strangers lost in night,
Casting shadows, pure and bright.

Pathways glow where footsteps lead,
Illuminating hearts that heed.
In the winter's calm delight,
Lanterns shine amidst the white.

A Blanket of Light

Gentle dawn with colors beam,
Waking worlds from slumber's dream.
A golden wash across the land,
Nature's brush, a soft, warm hand.

Clouds of pink and lavender hue,
Whisper promises, pure and true.
As daylight dawns, shadows take flight,
Wrapped in warmth, a blanket of light.

Shimmering Shadows

In the twilight's soft embrace,
Whispers dance with grace.
Flickering light and dark,
Create a secret spark.

Underneath the silver trees,
Echoes ride the breeze.
Mysterious forms unite,
Veiled in soft moonlight.

The Beacon's Embrace

A lighthouse stands so tall,
Guiding ships through squall.
With its warm, steady glow,
It beckons them below.

Waves crash on the stones,
Whispers of wayward tones.
In the storm's fierce embrace,
Hope finds a safe place.

Glowing Hearths and Heartstrings

In the heart of winter nights,
Fires crackle, share delights.
Among friends, laughter roars,
As the warmth forever pours.

Hand in hand, stories flow,
Time seems to gently slow.
With every flickering flame,
We bind our souls the same.

Embracing the Chill

Frosty breath in morning air,
Crisp and bright, a world so fair.
Blankets wrapped, snug and tight,
Hearts are warmed in pure delight.

Snowflakes dance like dreams alight,
Quiet paths in purest white.
Together we brave the cold,
In these moments, warmth unfolds.

Dance of the Flickering Flame

In the hearth, the shadows play,
A vibrant dance, night turns to day.
Whispers glow, the embers sing,
Life ignites in the warmth they bring.

Against the cold, they sway and spin,
A flicker bright, where warmth begins.
Dancing dreams in a cozy glow,
As time drifts on, the fire flows.

Each spark a tale, each glow a past,
Moments fleeting, yet they last.
In the heart, the flicker thrives,
In the dance, the spirit strives.

Soft Gleam Within the Dark

In the night, a gentle light,
Guiding hearts through endless fright.
Softly gleam the stars above,
Whispers of a distant love.

Shadows stretch and silence falls,
A soothing touch the night enthralls.
With every glimmer, hope does rise,
A promise held in moonlit skies.

Embrace the stillness, breathe it in,
Each soft gleam, a new begin.
In the dark, we find our way,
A beacon bright, come what may.

Hearthstone Serenades

By the fire, tales unfold,
Hearthstone sounds, warmth to behold.
Each crackle sings, each pop resounds,
In the glow, where peace abounds.

Voices mingle, stories shared,
In the light, love's memory bared.
Melodies dance in the flickering haze,
As we weave through laughter's maze.

Hands held close, hearts entwined,
In the serenade, joy we find.
With every note, a bond is sealed,
In the hearth, our lives revealed.

A Haven from the Frigid Boughs

Amidst the chill, the branches sway,
A haven found, where we can stay.
With walls of warmth, we nestle tight,
In our refuge, shadows take flight.

The world outside, so harsh, so cold,
Inside, the stories of love unfold.
A shelter soft against the storm,
In this embrace, our spirits warm.

Frost may bite at wooden frames,
But here, we kindle love's bright flames.
In every breath, a promise shared,
A haven built, where hearts have dared.

A Symphony of Soft Illuminations

In twilight's embrace, the lanterns glow,
Soft whispers of light in the evening's flow.
Stars twinkle gently, a celestial song,
A symphony playing, where dreams belong.

Shadows dance lightly, beneath the trees,
With flickers of warmth, carried by breeze.
The night wraps us close in a silken caress,
In every soft glow, we find our bliss.

The Winter's Secret Light

In the hush of the snow, a light hides away,
Whispering secrets in the chill of the day.
Icicles glisten like jewels in the night,
Each breath a cloud in the winter's white.

Softly it glimmers, in frost's gentle hold,
Stories of warmth, in the bitter and cold.
Together we gather, in a world made of dreams,
With winter's own light, bursting at the seams.

Glorious Glows of Coziness

A fire crackles softly, bright orange and red,
While shadows retreat from the warmth of our bed.
Blankets wrapped snugly, we cherish the night,
Glorious glows of coziness, holding us tight.

Cinnamon dances in the air, a sweet scent,
Each moment together, a treasure well spent.
Laughter and stories fill the room with delight,
In the glow of the evening, everything feels right.

Flickers of Joy in the Frost

Amidst the cold, joy begins to spark,
With flickers of warmth igniting the dark.
Children are laughing, their breath a soft mist,
In the heart of the frost, no moments are missed.

With every snowflake, a wish takes its flight,
Chasing the moon in the stillness of night.
In the chill of the air, our spirits arise,
Flickers of joy dance beneath winter skies.

Warmth Within Winter's Embrace

Snowflakes dance on frosty air,
Whispers of calm fill the night.
Inside, the fire glows so bright,
Hearts warm beneath winter's glare.

Laughter echoes through the hall,
Bundled close in soft blankets.
Outside, the chilling wind wails,
Yet inside, love breaks the fall.

Hot cocoa swirls in our hands,
Stories shared by the bright light.
Memories made in the quiet,
Together, we make our plans.

As the world turns white with frost,
We find joy in the embrace.
Winter's chill can never chase,
The warmth inside, never lost.

Golden Rays Beneath a Gray Sky

Overcast clouds hang so low,
Yet, rays break through with a glow.
The earth awakens from its rest,
In these moments, we are blessed.

Fields bathe in a golden hue,
While flowers bend in morning dew.
Life's beauty shines through the gloom,
A promise of brightness to bloom.

Children laugh beneath the trees,
As shadows chase along the breeze.
With every step, there's a spark,
Of warmth igniting in the dark.

Beneath the sky, we lift our gaze,
In the light, we find our ways.
Through the clouds, we see the grace,
Of golden rays in nature's embrace.

Ember Embrace of Night

Stars twinkle in the deep blue air,
The world grows quiet, dreams take flight.
In the silence, we find our share,
Of warmth held close in the night.

Crickets sing their evening song,
A melody soft, a tranquil call.
In the stillness, we feel so strong,
Together, we've conquered it all.

The fire crackles, a gentle spark,
Its dance brings comfort, warm and bright.
As shadows linger, we leave our mark,
In the ember's embrace, we delight.

Whispers of hopes drift like mist,
Under the watchful moon's embrace.
In this haven, we cannot resist,
The warmth found in the night's soft space.

Nocturnal Warmth

In the hush of twilight's glow,
Night wraps us in a gentle shroud.
Beneath the stars, our spirits grow,
In serene peace, we feel so proud.

The air is thick with sweet perfume,
Of blossoms open in the dark.
They whisper secrets, soft as loom,
Crafting dreams that leave a mark.

With every breath, a miracle,
The world seems held in starlit grace.
In the night, our hearts are full,
Finding warmth in this sacred space.

As shadows dance, we find our way,
With love illuminated bright.
In the night's embrace, we stay,
Nocturnal warmth fuels our flight.

The Soft Glow of Unseen Bonds

In shadows deep where whispers dwell,
A light emerges, gentle as a spell.
It weaves through hearts, unnoticed yet bright,
Binding us close, a warm, soft light.

In laughter shared and secrets told,
The unseen bonds, a treasure to hold.
Though miles apart, we feel the tie,
A glowing thread that will never die.

Through storms we weather, through trials we face,
These bonds remain a sacred space.
With every heartbeat, a silent call,
A soft glow that embraces us all.

Joy's Reflection on Frostbitten Land

Upon the ground, a shimmer bright,
Joy dances lightly, pure delight.
In every flake that falls from skies,
A spark of warmth beneath the lies.

The trees stand still, in frosty grace,
Each branch adorned, a jeweled place.
In icy breath, a promise grows,
Of life renewed when sunlight shows.

With laughter echoing through the chill,
We chase the frost, our hearts to fill.
In winter's clutch, we find a song,
A reflection of joy that lingers long.

A Safe Harbor of Light and Love

When storms arise and shadows creep,
A harbor waits, our hearts to keep.
In soft embraces, we find our rest,
A refuge built, where love is blessed.

The waves may crash, the winds may howl,
But in this place, no need to prowl.
With every tear that we have cried,
We find our shelter side by side.

In laughter's echo, in sorrow's shade,
The light of love will never fade.
With open arms, we welcome fate,
A safe harbor where dreams await.

Embracing the Night's Tender Luminescence

As twilight falls, the stars align,
A whispered hush, the world divine.
With gentle breaths, the night unfolds,
A tender glow that softly holds.

In shadows deep, where secrets lie,
We dance beneath the velvet sky.
Each flicker sings a lullaby,
Embracing dreams as they drift by.

In quiet moments, hearts entwine,
Within the night, our souls align.
A luminescent, soothing balm,
In darkness wrapped, we find our calm.

A Toast to the Frostbite

In winter's chill, we gather near,
With laughter bright, we shed our fear.
A toast to frost that bites the air,
In warmth of hearts, we find our care.

Snowflakes dance on frozen streams,
The world aglow with silver dreams.
With every sip, we feel alive,
In winter's hold, we thrive and strive.

Let fires crackle, stories flow,
To frosty nights, our spirits glow.
In every chill, a bond is made,
A toast to frost, our plans conveyed.

So lift your glass, let joy ignite,
Embrace the frost, our hearts take flight.
Through icy paths, we boldly tread,
A toast to life, where love is spread.

Luminous Echoes of the Night

Stars like diamonds fill the sky,
In the stillness, dreams can fly.
The moonlight whispers soft and clear,
Luminous echoes, drawing near.

In shadows deep, we find our way,
Through night's embrace, we dance till day.
With every step, the spirits gleam,
A tapestry of light, we dream.

As night unfolds its velvet cloak,
Each heartbeat sings, each silence spoke.
In every breath, the cosmos hums,
Luminous echoes, where wonder comes.

So lose yourself in starlit grace,
Find solace in this sacred space.
In whispered dreams, our souls unite,
In luminous echoes of the night.

Sanctuary of the Flame

In the heart of darkness, a spark ignites,
With warmth and comfort, it invites.
A sanctuary where spirits rise,
In flickering light, the past complies.

The flame dances, shadows play,
In its embrace, we find our way.
Stories shared, the past revealed,
In sanctuary, our wounds are healed.

With every glow, hope finds its voice,
In swirling embers, we rejoice.
Gathered together, hand in hand,
In the warmth of fire, we make our stand.

So let the flames forever shine,
In our hearts, a bond divine.
A sanctuary where dreams proclaim,
In unity, we fan the flame.

Twilight's Gentle Embrace

As daylight fades to twilight's tune,
The world is wrapped in softened gloom.
A gentle hush, the air turns sweet,
In twilight's arms, our hearts will meet.

The horizon blushes, colors blend,
A fleeting moment, it won't suspend.
In twilight's grasp, we breathe the still,
As time surrenders to night's warm thrill.

With whispers low, the stars appear,
In twilight's glow, we shed our fear.
Each cherished glance, a memory made,
In golden light, our dreams cascade.

So linger here, let moments tease,
In twilight's embrace, our souls find ease.
With every heartbeat, life's sweet grace,
In twilight's glow, our hearts embrace.

Lanterns of the Soul

In the quiet of the night,
Soft whispers guide our way,
Lanterns glowing in the dark,
Illuminating hearts that sway.

Each flicker tells a tale,
Of dreams that rise and fall,
Shadows dance in gentle light,
Echoes of a distant call.

Threads of hope intertwine,
With every soul we meet,
A tapestry of warmth,
Lifelines woven, bittersweet.

Together we will shine,
In this sacred, warm embrace,
Lanterns of the soul will glow,
Guiding us through time and space.

The Warmth We Carry

Underneath a starry sky,
Hearts beat soft and slow,
The warmth we carry deep inside,
A fire that always glows.

Silent moments shared as one,
Hands held tight in trust,
In the darkest of the night,
It's love that turns to dust.

Through the storms and through the rain,
We find strength in our tears,
For the warmth we carry close,
Will guide us through our fears.

With every step we take,
The light will never fade,
In the embrace of you and me,
A home that's gently made.

Illumined Solitude

In solitude we find our peace,
A quiet space to breathe,
Thoughts like ripples on the sea,
In stillness, we believe.

The stars blink down, so far away,
Yet close enough to feel,
Whispers of the universe,
In silence, they reveal.

Each moment stretches like the dawn,
Colors blend and merge,
Illumined solitude, a friend,
In this quiet surge.

Here among the shadows cast,
We learn to be alone,
In the echoes of our mind,
We find ourselves, our own.

Dancing Flames of Solace

In the hearth where embers glow,
Dancing flames with grace,
They sway and twist like memories,
Filling up the space.

A warmth that wraps around us tight,
In the cold, cutting night,
Each flicker tells a story long,
Of love's unyielding might.

With every crack and gentle pop,
We find comfort in the blaze,
Dancing flames of solace rise,
Guiding us through the haze.

So let us sit and share this glow,
As laughter breaks the chill,
In the rhythm of our hearts,
We dance, we dare, we will.

Whispered Light in the Cold

In the frost where shadows lie,
A gentle glow begins to sigh.
Soft whispers dance on winter's breath,
A tender warmth defying death.

Stars above in silent gaze,
Guide the lost through snowy haze.
In the night, the spirits play,
While dreams of warmth drift far away.

Each flicker tells a story old,
Of love and hope in every fold.
In the stillness, hearts unfold,
Embraced by light as warmth takes hold.

Fireside Whispers

By the flames, we find our voice,
In the crackle, sparks rejoice.
Tales of yore, secrets spun,
In amber glow, we come undone.

Roaring fire in cozy nest,
Wraps us close, in warmth we're blessed.
With every log that breaks apart,
Fireside whispers warm the heart.

Eyes aglow, with love ignited,
In this moment, we're united.
The world outside fades far away,
In this haven, here we stay.

Embered Hearts

In quietude, our souls ignite,
With embers glowing through the night.
Two hearts beating, side by side,
In love's embrace, we shall abide.

Silhouettes in flickering light,
Whispers shared, futures bright.
The warmth we weave, a sacred space,
In every glance, a soft embrace.

Through trials faced and storms we've braved,
In this glow, we have been saved.
Embered hearts, forever bold,
In each other's arms, the light unfolds.

Glowing Hearths of Solitude

Within the solitude we find,
Hearths aglow, our hearts aligned.
In the quiet, comfort flows,
As time slows down, the spirit grows.

Flames leap high, shadows dance,
In this space, there's a chance.
To ponder dreams and past regret,
In glowing light, we can reset.

Silence deepens, thoughts reside,
In isolation, truth can hide.
Yet in this warmth, we come alive,
With every flicker, we revive.

Refuges of Light in the Night

Amidst the shadows, stars appear,
Whispering dreams for all to hear.
Lanterns flicker, hope ignites,
Guiding wandering souls through nights.

In deep darkness, warmth arrives,
A gentle touch that soothes and thrives.
Safe havens beckon, bright and true,
Embracing all in light's warm hue.

Silent prayers drift through the dark,
Each shimmer a faint, guiding spark.
The moon's silver beams softly play,
Chasing the fears of yesterday.

A refuge found in every glow,
Where hearts can rest and kindness flow.
Through glistening paths, we stand as one,
Illuminated by the rising sun.

Hearth and Haven in a Winter Wonderland

Snowflakes dance in the chilly air,
Blanketing the earth with gentle care.
The hearth's warm crackle sings to me,
In this wonderland, I feel so free.

Icicles hang like jewels aglow,
Nature's beauty in a pristine show.
Fireside whispers invite the heart,
As cozy blankets become a part.

Outside the world is crisp and bright,
Inside, the warmth feels just right.
Glistening trees adorn the night,
In the embrace of soft, golden light.

In this haven, I find my peace,
As winter's chill begins to cease.
Moments linger, time stands still,
Wrapped in warmth, the heart can fill.

The Melody of Glistening Rays

Morning breaks with a gentle blaze,
Softly weaving through the haze.
Sunrise whispers, a sweet refrain,
Awakening life with joy unchained.

The dew drips from blades of green,
Nature's jewels, gracefully seen.
Birds sing sweetly, a vibrant tune,
Every note a gift from June.

Glistening rays on water play,
Cascading light in joyful display.
Each shimmer tells stories old,
Of dreams, of journeys yet untold.

Together we bask in this glow,
As melodies of morning flow.
The world awakens, hearts unite,
In the melody of dawn's first light.

Enchanted by the Hearth's Glow

In a cabin, warm and bright,
Crackling flames dance in the night.
The hearth glows with a tender light,
Wrapping us close, holding us tight.

Stories shared, laughter flows,
Each moment cherished, love just grows.
As shadows flicker on the wall,
Together we rise, together we fall.

Outside the winter winds may wail,
But in here, warmth will prevail.
With every ember, we find delight,
Enchanted by the hearth's warm light.

So let the world beyond be cold,
In this haven, we are bold.
Hearts united in glowing cheer,
Forever cherished, ever near.

The Kindling of Gentle Nights

In the hush of twilight's glow,
Stars begin their gentle show,
Whispers dance on the cool breeze,
Painting dreams among the trees.

Fires crackle, stories unfold,
Magic spun from embers bold,
Night's embrace wraps tender and tight,
Guiding souls through the soft light.

Shadows play on the wall's grace,
Memories linger in this space,
Hearts entwined, lost in delight,
In the kindling of gentle nights.

Radiant Refuge from the Blasts

Winter winds may howl and fight,
But inside, warmth feels so right,
A haven built with love and care,
Radiance shines through the air.

Candles flicker, shadows dance,
Filling hearts with sweet romance,
Laughter lingers, spirits soar,
Within this refuge, we explore.

Together, we face the cold's bite,
In our fortress of soft light,
All worries fade, the world is vast,
Here we find peace, unsurpassed.

Hearthside Tales Under Snowfall

Snowflakes drift like whispered dreams,
Falling softly, it seems,
By the hearth, the fire glows,
Casting tales that love bestows.

Voices blend in a cozy hum,
Timeless stories now begun,
Characters dance in embers' light,
Each word a spark, igniting night.

The world outside is cold and grey,
Within, we linger, hearts at play,
Hearthside memories take their flight,
Under snow's gentle, pure white.

Light's Embrace on Frosty Evenings

As daylight wanes and shadows creep,
Frosty evenings coax us deep,
Light's embrace, a comforting hold,
Warming tales of ages old.

Through the window, the stars appear,
A cosmic dance that draws us near,
With every flicker, hope ignites,
Transforming chill into delights.

Sipping cocoa, time stands still,
Heartfelt laughter warms the chill,
In this glow, worries release,
Finding joy, we feel true peace.

Embered Reveries in the Cold

In shadows deep, where silence sighs,
Whispers dance beneath the skies.
Flickers warm in icy air,
Dreams alight, beyond despair.

Stars above, like embers glow,
Hearts entwined in winter's flow.
Memories wrapped in quilted night,
Soft embraces hold us tight.

The Radiance That Defies Chill

Through frosted panes, the light breaks free,
Casting warmth, a gentle plea.
In every breath, a spark ignites,
Against the cold, the spirit fights.

Fires glow in hearts anew,
Illuminating paths we pursue.
When winter's grip tries to prevail,
Hope inside will never pale.

Dewy Light on Snowy Eves

In tender dawn, the world aglow,
Dewdrops dance on fields of snow.
Each crystal spark, a fleeting dream,
Nature's breath, a flawless seam.

As daylight breaks, the chill subsides,
In every corner, beauty hides.
With whispers soft, the day awakes,
In snowy arms, the heart remakes.

Twilight's Glimmer of Hope

As twilight falls, the sky transforms,
A canvas rich with quiet forms.
Each fading ray, a lullaby,
Promises whispered in the by.

In shadows cast by evening's grace,
We find a warm, familiar space.
With every star, a wish takes flight,
In twilight's glow, we stand upright.

Fireside Whispers

The crackling flames softly dance,
As shadows play in a warm trance.
Whispers ride the gentle breeze,
Tales of old and memories.

A cozy nook where hearts convene,
Stories shared, a tranquil scene.
Embers glow with a tender light,
Silhouettes brush the edges of night.

Hot cocoa warms each loving hand,
Together as we softly stand.
The world outside begins to freeze,
Inside, we find a heart's reprise.

Laughter echoes through the air,
Moments treasured, beyond compare.
Fireside whispers, love's sweet tune,
Comfort found beneath the moon.

Embered Dreams

In the night, the embers gleam,
Casting visions, a sweet dream.
Burning bright with hopeful glow,
Leading where our wishes flow.

Stars above begin to wink,
As we share the thoughts we think.
Whispers shared through softest sighs,
With every breath, our spirits rise.

A journey wrapped in warmth and light,
Adventures spark beneath the night.
With every flicker, dreams ignite,
A promise held in shared delight.

Together we create a world,
With every story, joy unfurled.
Embered dreams in twilight's air,
A tapestry of love we share.

Glow Against the Frost

Outside, the air is biting cold,
Yet inside, warmth begins to hold.
A gentle glow against the frost,
In the embrace of love, we're lost.

Candles dance with gold and flame,
Every flicker whispers a name.
Frozen windows, a silver veil,
Within these walls, we will not fail.

Hot cider warms our souls and hearts,
As laughter fills the silent parts.
In this refuge, we are free,
Glow against the frost, just you and me.

As snowflakes fall, we sit and weave,
A tapestry that won't deceive.
In every glance, there's a spark,
Igniting passion in the dark.

Hearthside Serenade

By the hearth, the fire glows,
In its warmth, our friendship grows.
A serenade of love and cheer,
In this moment, I hold you near.

Softly hum a lullaby,
As embers dance and dreams float by.
The world outside is cold and grim,
But here, our hearts will never dim.

Each story spun, a dance of light,
As shadows twirl in the peaceful night.
With every word and gentle tune,
Our souls unite beneath the moon.

So let the fire crackle loud,
In this soft glow, we are proud.
Together, we shall softly sing,
In hearthside serenade, love's offering.

Resilience of Radiant Dreams

In shadows deep, we find our way,
Holding tight to hopes that sway.
With every stumble, we rise anew,
A spark inside, forever true.

Through storms we march, with hearts so bold,
Embers of courage, stories told.
We weave our fate with threads of light,
Resilient souls that shine so bright.

Though challenges may test our might,
Together we stand, ready to fight.
Among the stars, our dreams take flight,
In unity, we find our sight.

So lift your voice, let laughter ring,
In the dance of life, we are the spring.
For through the struggle, love redeems,
In the heart's embrace, reside our dreams.

Whispered Warmth Beneath Silver Skies

Under the moon's soft, gentle glow,
Whispers of twilight, secrets flow.
Wrapped in the night, the world feels right,
Hearts entwined, a timeless sight.

Amidst the stars, our dreams arise,
Flickering lights in endless skies.
With every breath, the night inspires,
A tender warmth that never tires.

The cool night air cradles our sighs,
In silence shared, the heart complies.
With open arms, we greet the dawn,
In whispered warmth, we carry on.

So let us dance beneath the light,
In the embrace of the friendly night.
As silver skies envelop our dreams,
In love, we find the purest themes.

The Fire's Gentle Lullaby

In the hearth's glow, stories unfold,
With whispers soft, and embers gold.
A crackling tune, a soothing sound,
In the fire's heart, peace is found.

It wraps us close, a cozy embrace,
Each flicker tells of time and space.
Gathered together, we find our way,
To the gentle lull of the fire's play.

Through smoky trails and warm delight,
We dream together, a sacred night.
As shadows dance upon the wall,
In the fire's warmth, we feel it all.

Let the lullaby carry us high,
On wings of warmth, beneath the sky.
For as long as the flames burn bright,
In their song, we take our flight.

Celestial Comforts in Frosty Embrace

In winter's grip, the world holds still,
A blanket of white, on every hill.
Beneath the stars, the night feels pure,
In frosty breath, we find the cure.

The hush of snow, a gentle sigh,
Wrapped in comfort, we dare to fly.
With each cool gust, dreams take their place,
In nature's lull, we find our grace.

Among the flakes that swirl and gleam,
We drink the warmth of winter's dream.
With tinsel lights, our hearts ignite,
A celestial charm in the frosty night.

So gather close, in this embrace,
Find solace in the quiet space.
In the chill, the soul finds calm,
With celestial comforts, we are warm.

Cozy Corners of the Heart

In quiet nooks where whispers dwell,
Soft cushions cradle tales to tell.
A gentle fire, the warmth it shares,
Speaks to the soul in tender cares.

The curtains sway with evening's sigh,
As shadows dance beneath the sky.
With every laugh, a memory makes,
In cozy corners, love awakes.

A teacup shared, reflections blend,
In these small spaces, hearts transcend.
The world outside may fade away,
Inside, we find our place to stay.

So let us linger, hand in hand,
In cozy corners, understand.
Together, we ignite the spark,
That keeps us warm when days grow dark.

Flickers Against the Cold

The candle's light begins to sway,
As winter's chill holds night at bay.
Its golden glow, a gentle guide,
Through frosty winds, we choose to bide.

Each flicker tells a story clear,
Of moments shared, of those held dear.
As snowflakes fall, like dreams they lay,
In cozy warmth, we find our way.

The hearth's embrace, a soothing balm,
In every flicker, peace and calm.
Against the cold, we stand as one,
With hearts aflame, till night is done.

Let shadows dance upon the wall,
As laughter echoes, sweet and small.
Through flickers bright, we'll carry light,
In coldest times, our love ignites.

Illuminated Dreams in Frost

Beneath the stars where frosty winds,
Whisper soft secrets, night rescinds.
In dreams illuminated, we roam,
Through winter's hush, we find our home.

A tapestry of silver plays,
On vacant paths and moonlit ways.
With every chill, a warmth we seek,
In dreams alive, our spirits peak.

The frosted panes, a canvas bright,
Hold stories spun in soft moonlight.
With every breath, we melt the gloom,
Illuminated dreams in bloom.

So close your eyes, let visions flow,
Through winter's grasp, our hearts will glow.
In a world adorned with ice and cheer,
Illuminated dreams draw near.

The Glow of Comforting Shadows

In the depth of night, shadows breathe,
A comforting glow, like a silken wreath.
Wrapped in warmth, we find our place,
As darkness softens, a gentle embrace.

With whispered tales and soothing tones,
The glow of shadows, where love condones.
Each flicker dances, a story spun,
In the heart's refuge, we are one.

Together we sit, as time drifts by,
In the glow of comfort, under starlit sky.
With every heartbeat, the world stands still,
In shadows' embrace, we are filled.

So let the night wrap us tight,
In comforting shadows, we find our light.
With every breath, a promise made,
In the glow of love, we're not afraid.

The Gentle Flicker of Remembrance

In the twilight of our dreams, we find,
Soft whispers of the past unwind.
Echoes of laughter, shadows of light,
A tender reminder, memories bright.

Time drifts softly like a feathered sigh,
Carried by winds where thoughts can fly.
In the heart's treasure chest, they stay,
The gentle flicker, guiding the way.

Each moment cherished, a star in the night,
Illuminates our journey, holding us tight.
Through the corridors of time we roam,
In the flicker of remembrance, we find our home.

So let us cherish the warmth we seek,
In every memory, in every peek.
For though the light may often wane,
The gentle flicker remains, unchained.

Glow Beyond the Frosty Veil

In icy whispers, silence speaks,
A world adorned in winter's peaks.
Yet beneath the frost, life gently glows,
Hidden warmth that softly flows.

The dawn breaks through with golden grace,
Chasing shadows, a warm embrace.
As snowflakes dance and twirl in air,
A spark ignites, beyond despair.

In gardens dressed in silver white,
The hope of spring begins to write.
With every breath, the chill does fade,
Revealing dreams that time has made.

Embrace the glow that flickers bright,
A beacon shining through the night.
For even in the coldest times,
Hope's gentle pulse forever climbs.

Radiant Reflections in Stillness

Amid the quiet, stillness lies,
A mirror to the world, the skies.
Through tranquil waters, light does play,
In radiant reflections, dreams sway.

Like whispered secrets long forgone,
In calm serenity, we are drawn.
Each ripple tells a tale untold,
In the heart's canvas, the soul unfolds.

When dusk descends and shadows blend,
Life's fleeting moments softly bend.
In every glimmer, memories gleam,
Radiant reflections, a waking dream.

Hold dear the calm within your heart,
For in stillness, beauty finds its part.
In every pause, let your spirit fly,
In radiant reflections, we learn to cry.

The Hearth's Dance of Warmth

By the hearth's glow, we gather near,
Where stories echo, voices clear.
Flames in a dance, a wild embrace,
Warmth envelops, time slows its pace.

Each crackle sings a lullaby sweet,
Bringing together hearts in a beat.
In the flickering light, shadows play,
In the warmth of the hearth, we find our way.

The world outside, a chilly maze,
Yet in this circle, love's bright blaze.
As laughter lingers and spirits soar,
The hearth's dance ignites forevermore.

So let us hold each moment tight,
As embers glow in the deepening night.
For in this warmth, we truly belong,
In the hearth's embrace, we sing our song.

Comfort in Radiant Flickers

In the dim glow of the night,
Flickers warm the heart with ease.
Whispers of hope take their flight,
As shadows dance in gentle breeze.

A candle's flame, a tender spark,
Guides the lost through darkened ways.
Each flicker sings a quiet lark,
Illuminating distant days.

Beneath the stars, our dreams ignite,
Embers glowing with sweet delight.
In radiant warmth, we find our place,
In every flicker, a soft embrace.

Hold tight to this comforting light,
For in each glow, love's presence stays.
Through radiant flickers of the night,
We find our peace in endless rays.

Sledding Through Glowing Memories

Snowflakes fall like dreams untold,
Sleds rush down with joyful screams.
In winter's arms, we feel so bold,
Chasing the warmth of childhood dreams.

Laughter echoes, spirits soar,
Through drifts of white, we dance and glide.
Each sled ride opens memory's door,
As the past and present coincide.

Cold cheeks flush with rosy hue,
Frosty air fills our lungs with cheer.
With every turn, the world feels new,
In glowing memories, we persevere.

So let us sled, let joy increase,
On winter's canvas, we leave our mark.
Through glowing memories, we find peace,
As laughter echoes after dark.

A Twinkle in the Frost

Morning light coats the world in grace,
Each blade of grass adorned with ice.
A twinkle glows in nature's face,
A reminder of winter's paradise.

In the quiet, a soft embrace,
Pine trees wear their snowy crowns.
Every crystal finds its place,
As joy in silence gently drowns.

Footsteps crunch on frosted ground,
Whispers float in the chilly air.
In each twinkle, beauty's found,
A world transformed, beyond compare.

Hold close this magic, feel it rise,
A twinkle's glow within our hearts.
In the frost, we see the skies,
As winter's charm forever starts.

Serene Gleams of Life

In the stillness of the dawn,
Gentle glimmers softly gleam.
Awakening to a world's yawn,
Life unfolds like a tender dream.

Leaves dance lightly in the breeze,
Sunlight filters through the trees.
Each moment's grace, a quiet tease,
In nature's arms, we feel at ease.

Rippling waters reflect the sky,
Whispers of peace in every flow.
Here in this space, we gaze and sigh,
As serene gleams of life bestow.

Embrace the warmth of every ray,
In simplicity, joy resides.
Serene gleams guide us through the day,
As love and light forever abides.

Lanterns in the Snow

Soft glow dances on white ground,
Whispers of warmth all around.
Each lantern a beacon, a friend,
Guiding us home, where love transcends.

In the stillness, magic unfolds,
Stories of hope in the chill as told.
Together we gather, hearts aligned,
In the embrace of the night, we find.

Frosted breaths rise in the air,
Hand in hand, no room for despair.
Through the darkness, we light the way,
Lanterns in snow, forever we stay.

With every flicker, our spirits soar,
In a world of white, we search for more.
Hope shines bright, like stars above,
Guiding us always, wrapped in love.

Flickering Resilience

In the silence, shadows sway,
Flickering flames at the end of the day.
Each spark a note of silent song,
Resilience whispers, 'You belong.'

Though winds may howl, we stand our ground,
In the darkness, strength is found.
With every challenge, we ignite,
A dance of shadows, bold and bright.

Echoes of courage, we carry on,
Through trials faced, new dawns are drawn.
Flickering lights, our hearts ignite,
Together we rise, into the night.

In the smallest glow, we find our way,
Guided by love, come what may.
Through every storm, we'll fiercely glow,
Flickering resilience, forever we'll show.

Radiance Amidst the Cold

Amidst the frost, a warm embrace,
Radiance lights the darkest space.
Each beam of light, a thread of grace,
Holding us close in this vast place.

The chill may bite, the night be long,
But in our hearts, we sing a song.
Of warmth and hope that won't grow dim,
Together, forever, we'll stand with whim.

Stars sprinkle the sky like dreams untold,
In this sacred night, we break the mold.
Hand in hand, we create our way,
Radiance glimmers, guiding our stay.

In the depths of winter, spirits rise,
With each shared smile, love never dies.
Through every shadow, we remain bold,
Finding radiance amidst the cold.

Comfort in Candlelight

In the quiet glow, we gather near,
Candlelight flickers, chasing fear.
A dance of shadows on the wall,
In this moment, we share it all.

Kindred spirits, hearts entwined,
In the warmth, a love defined.
Each flame a story, whispered soft,
Comfort found, rising aloft.

The world outside may be harsh and gray,
But here in light, we find our way.
Each candle a promise, a gentle hug,
Filling the space, a heartwarming tug.

As the winds outside begin to howl,
We sit together, beneath the prowl.
Comfort in candlelight, our souls ignite,
In this embrace, we shine so bright.

The Light Within an Icy Veil

Behind the frost, there glows a spark,
A warmth that whispers in the dark.
Beneath the surface, dreams align,
As hope unfurls like a sweet vine.

In shadows cast by frozen night,
The heart still beats, a source of light.
Through tender cracks, bright colors burst,
Reminding us of love's great thirst.

Each breath a promise, soft yet clear,
A gentle pull to draw us near.
In winter's grasp, we find our way,
As springtime blooms within the gray.

For even when the cold winds wail,
There's a light that breaks the icy veil.
We hold the truth within our core,
That love, once kindled, will restore.

Flickering Promises of Tomorrow

In twilight's grasp, the stars ignite,
Each flicker dances, a beacon bright.
The night unfolds, a canvas wide,
Where dreams reside and fears subside.

With every pulse, the darkness fades,
New paths emerge through the thickest shades.
A whispered vow, a dreamer's quest,
To seek the dawn, to feel the best.

The flame within will always guide,
Through tempest storms and ocean tides.
With open hearts, we chase the day,
And let tomorrow light the way.

For promises, though soft they seem,
Can weave the thread of every dream.
With hope in hand, we'll surely borrow,
The flickering promises of tomorrow.

Echoes of Light in Stillness

In silence deep, the echoes play,
A symphony of light's ballet.
Each note, a whisper from the sky,
Where dreams weave in and quietly fly.

The world around may seem to pause,
Yet here we find our truest cause.
In stillness lies a vibrant hue,
An unseen force that pulls us through.

Each heartbeat speaks, a gentle thrum,
A call to rise, to be and become.
Within the calm, our spirits dance,
Embracing life's sweet, quiet chance.

In echoes soft, we find our grace,
The light within this sacred space.
Every moment, pure and bright,
Is an echo of love's endless light.

Shimmering Solace in a Cold World

In bitter winds, we seek a flame,
A tender spark to shield our name.
Through icy strokes, our hearts still gleam,
In this harsh world, we find our dream.

With every breath, we share our light,
A warmth that cuts through the deepest night.
Together, strong, we face the chill,
In love's embrace, we find the will.

Each whisper shared, a soft embrace,
As shimmering solace finds its place.
In darkest hours, we stand as one,
Our hearts aglow, like the morning sun.

So let the world be cold and stark,
We'll hold the flame, ignite the spark.
For in our bond, we'll bravely face,
The shimmering solace, our saving grace.

Flickering Dreams of Timeless Nights

In silent whispers, dreams take flight,
Under the blanket of soft starlight.
Each flicker a hope, each sparkle a sigh,
Timeless moments in the midnight sky.

The world hushed down, the clock stands still,
Where shadows dance, and hearts can feel.
In the crescent glow, our wishes bloom,
In flickering dreams, we find our room.

Beneath the moon's gaze, we intertwine,
Chasing the echoes, so divine.
Through endless night, our spirits soar,
In flickering dreams, forevermore.

Hand in hand, we chase what's lost,
Through timeless nights, we count the cost.
With every heartbeat, the night grows bright,
In flickering dreams, love takes its flight.

Illuminated Pathways to Joy

Upon the road where shadows fade,
Illuminated paths our hearts have made.
With every step, a joy unfolds,
A tapestry of stories that life beholds.

Through gardens bright and fields of gold,
We walk together, hand in hold.
The laughter rings like chimes in trees,
With each embrace, our spirits seize.

The sun arises, painting skies anew,
In the glowing dawn, hope breaks through.
As pathways twist, our spirits sing,
Illuminated joy, the light we bring.

From dusk till dawn, our journey flows,
Through every joy, our love still grows.
On illuminated roads, we stride,
In every moment, love is our guide.

Laughter Among Glowing Flames

Around the fire, stories shared,
Laughter dances, warmth is bared.
Glowing flames flicker in the night,
In the glow of friendship, hearts unite.

Each crackle sparks a tale to tell,
With every smile, we weave a spell.
The ember's glow brings peace within,
Among the flames, our joy begins.

With every laugh, the shadows fade,
In glowing warmth, memories made.
Around the fire, spirits soar high,
In laughter's embrace, we learn to fly.

As stars twinkle in the vast expanse,
We find our rhythm in night's dance.
In laughter's tune, our hearts reclaim,
The glowing flames, they call our name.

Shadows Cast by Celestial Light

Beneath the stars, shadows take form,
Whispers of night, a tranquil charm.
In celestial light, our fears unwind,
Shadows of hope, love intertwined.

The moon's embrace, a gentle guide,
Through darkened paths, we choose to stride.
Each shadow dances, each shape reveals,
In celestial light, our heart conspels.

As constellations paint the sky,
We share our dreams, just you and I.
Shadows cast long, but light is near,
In the cosmic glow, we hold what's dear.

Together we stand, under starlit dome,
In shadows and light, we make our home.
With every heartbeat, the night collides,
Shadows of love where the universe hides.

Frost-Kissed Luminescence

In the hush of winter's breath,
Snowflakes dance on twilight's edge,
Soft whispers weave a silver thread,
Capturing dreams where shadows dredge.

Moonlight glimmers on icy seas,
Each crest a world of sparkling light,
Crystals form with frozen ease,
A gentle glow against the night.

Beneath the branches draped in white,
Nature holds her breath in calm,
Frost-kissed scenes, a pure delight,
The world wrapped tight in winter's balm.

As dawn approaches, colors blend,
A canvas painted fresh and bright,
In every corner, beauty sends,
Frost-kissed luminescence ignites.

Flickers of Hope

In the heart of a quiet night,
Stars begin to softly gleam,
Each one a flicker, a tiny light,
Whispering promises like a dream.

Through the veils of doubt and fear,
Hope springs forth in gentle hues,
It dances close, always near,
A flame that flickers, never to lose.

When shadows stretch and darkness swells,
A spark ignites in souls grown tired,
Where whispers of resilience dwells,
Flickers of hope are always inspired.

Together we rise, hand in hand,
With each flicker, we find our way,
In the darkness, we boldly stand,
Embracing the dawn of a new day.

Solace Beneath the Stars

Underneath the vast expanse,
Where silence hums a gentle tune,
We find our peace in night's romance,
Wrapped tight beneath the silver moon.

Each twinkle tells a secret tale,
Of journeys taken, dreams fulfilled,
In stillness, we set our sails,
A canvas blank, our hearts distilled.

Breathe deeply the cool, crisp air,
Feel the weight of the world release,
In constellations, night lays bare,
A promise of unwavering peace.

So here we sit, lost in time,
With every star, we gently weave,
A tapestry of light and rhyme,
Solace found, in night we believe.

Illumination Through the Blizzards

As snowflakes whirl in wild parade,
The world transforms to white and gray,
In the cold, a warmth is laid,
Illumination finds its way.

Through blizzards fierce, through bitter chill,
A spark remains, a glowing flame,
With courage strong, we climb the hill,
For every storm douses not the same.

The heart persists, it learns to shine,
Each flurry lends a gentle grace,
In the darkest nights, we intertwine,
Embracing light in winter's embrace.

Each gust of wind, a whisper clear,
That echoes hope through frosted air,
Illumination strong and dear,
Through blizzards wild, we find our prayer.

Milton Keynes UK
Ingram Content Group UK Ltd.
UKHW021844151124
451262UK00014B/1291

9 789916 944271